DISCOVER THE DIFFERENCE

Shark and Dolphin

Rod Theodorou and Carole Telford

RIGBY
INTERACTIVE
LIBRARY

Printed in Britain

Library of Congress Cataloging-in-Publication Data
Theodorou, Rod.
      Shark and dolphin / Rod Theodorou and Carole Telford.
            p.   cm. — (Discover the difference)
      Includes index.
      Summary: Compares and contrasts the physical attributes, habits, and
      habitat of sharks and dolphins.
      ISBN 1-57572-101-5 (lib. bdg.)
      1. Sharks—Juvenile literature. 2. Dolphins—Juvenile literature. [1. Sharks.
      2. Dolphins.] I. Telford, Carole, 1961–   . II. Title. III. Series: Theodorou, Rod.
      Discover the difference.
      QL638.9.T48 1996
      597'.31—dc20   96-5554

Designed by Susan Clarke
Illustrations by Jeff Edwards

Acknowledgments
The publisher would like to thank the following for permission to reproduce photographs: James
Watt/Oxford Scientific Films, p. 4; P. Morris/Ardea London Ltd., p. 6 *top*; Marty Snyderman/Planet
Earth Pictures, p. 6 *bottom*; K. and L. Laidler/Ardea London Ltd., p. 7; Norbert Wu/NHPA, pp. 8, 16;
Ron and Valerie Taylor/Ardea London Ltd., pp. 3 *top*, 8 *bottom*, 10 *top*, 18 *top and bottom*; Francois
Gohier/ Ardea London Ltd., pp. 9, 15, 23; G.I. Bernard/ NHLA, p. 10 *bottom*; James Watt/Planet Earth
Pictures, p. 11; Flip Schulke/ Planet Earth Pictures, p. 12 *top*; Brian Pitkin/Planet Earth Pictures, p. 12;
T. Stephenson/ FLPA, p. 13 *top*; Ken Lucas/ Planet Earth Pictures p. 13 *bottom*; ANT/NHPA p. 14; Nick
Gordon/Ardea London Ltd., p. 17; Howard Hall/Oxford Scientific Films, pp. 19, 20 *middle and bottom*;
Tom McHugh/Oxford Scientific Films, p. 20 *top*; Marineland/FLPA, pp. 3 *bottom*, 21; Doug Perrine/
Planet Earth Pictures, p. 22.

Cover photographs reproduced with permission of Marty Snyderman/Planet Earth Pictures, *top*;
Ken Lucas, Planet Earth Pictures, *bottom*.

Every effort has been made to contact copyright holders of any material reproduced in this book. Any
omissions will be rectified in subsequent printings if notice is given to the publisher.

> **Note to the Reader**
> Some words in this book are printed in **bold** type. This indicates that the word is
> listed in the glossary on page 24. The glossary gives a brief explanation of words
> that may be new to you and tells you the page on which each word first appears.

Contents

Introduction

Sharks are fish. There are more than 350 **species** of shark. Some of them are huge, but many of them are quite small. At nine inches long, a fully grown pygmy shark could fit in the palm of your hand.

Sharks do not have a skeleton made from bone, like other fish do. Shark skeletons are made from a light, rubbery, white material called *cartilage*.

Many people think that sharks attack hundreds of people every year, but this is not true! Most species of shark are harmless. About 30 to 50 shark attacks are reported throughout the world each year. Far more people are killed by bees or in horse-riding accidents.

It's amazing!

A whale shark is as long as a fishing boat. One of these sharks can weigh as much as 20 tons and reach 50 feet long or more.

The whale shark is the biggest fish of all.

Dolphins may look like fish, but they are not. They are mammals, just like us. They breathe air, are warm-blooded, and feed their young with milk.

Dolphins are a type of small whale, as are porpoises. There are 37 different species of dolphin. The largest of them is the orca, or "killer whale." It grows up to 33 feet long.

Dolphins come in many sizes. Porpoises look like dolphins, but are smaller and have rounder beaks.

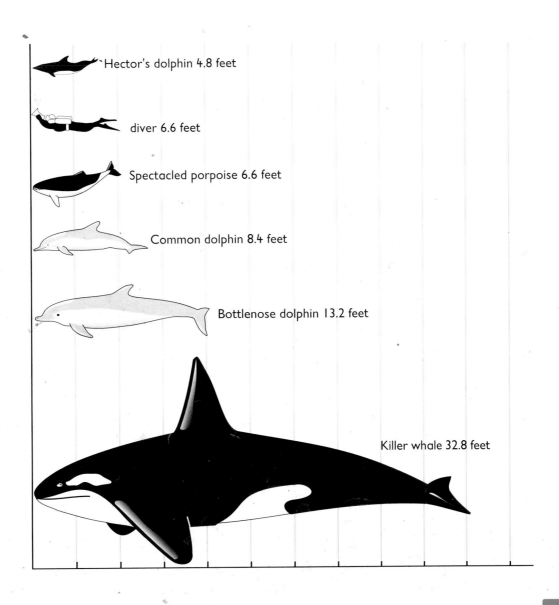

Hector's dolphin 4.8 feet

diver 6.6 feet

Spectacled porpoise 6.6 feet

Common dolphin 8.4 feet

Bottlenose dolphin 13.2 feet

Killer whale 32.8 feet

Habitat

Sharks live in all the world's oceans, especially in warmer waters. Some, like dogfish, live and feed on the ocean floor. Other sharks swim together in open waters, in schools. Hunting in schools gives them the best chance of catching fish. The really big sharks do not swim in schools. They spend all their lives hunting alone for large **prey** in the open sea.

Dogfish are small sharks that live in shallow coastal water.

Huge sharks, like the great white shark, hunt alone.

Dolphins live in oceans in many parts of the world. Some dolphins even live in rivers and lakes. Dolphins are social animals; they like to live in groups. There may be only a few dolphins in a group, or they can be part of a larger herd of up to 1,000 animals. Dolphins swim together, play together, and sometimes hunt fish together by herding them.

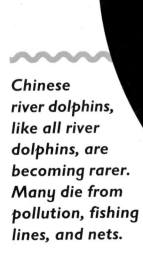

Chinese river dolphins, like all river dolphins, are becoming rarer. Many die from pollution, fishing lines, and nets.

Speed, Shape, and Color

Most sharks are **streamlined**, like torpedoes, so they can swim fast. Perhaps the fastest is the mako shark, which can swim as fast as 60 mph.

Not all sharks are gray. Angel sharks live on the ocean floor and can hide easily because they are the color of sand.

An angel shark hides in the sand.

The hammerhead shark has a strange head. Its eyes and nostrils are at the ends of the "hammer."

Dolphins can move faster by leaping out of the water.

It's amazing!
Killer whales are the fastest water mammal. They can swim at speeds of up to 40 mph!

Dolphins are also streamlined. They are fast swimmers, reaching speeds of up to 28 mph. Their shape makes them good acrobats, too. Dolphins can leap out of the water with ease.

Dolphins are usually a blue-gray color. This **camouflage** makes them difficult to see in deep water. It helps dolphins stay hidden from fish they are hunting and also from their enemies!

Skin

Like many other kinds of fish, sharks have **scales.**
However, shark scales are unusual. They are
small and very sharp, like tiny teeth This makes
shark skin very rough and protects the shark.
Divers can be badly grazed by brushing against
a shark.

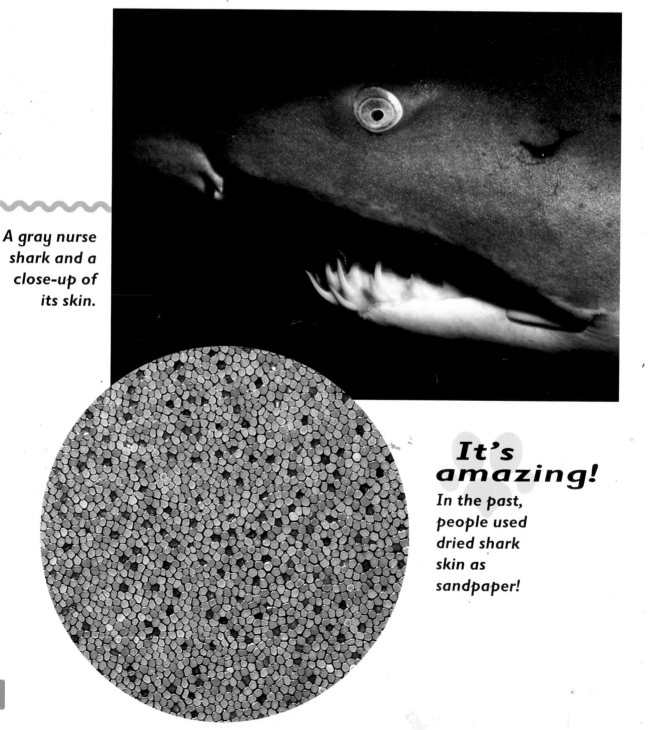

*A gray nurse
shark and a
close-up of
its skin.*

It's amazing!

*In the past,
people used
dried shark
skin as
sandpaper!*

Dolphins do not have scales. Instead they have smooth, soft, hairless skin. Dolphins shed their special outer layer of skin often. This means their skin is always in good condition, which helps the dolphin swim well. Under the skin is a layer of fat, called "blubber," that keeps them warm and also helps them float.

A dolphin's skin is covered with an oily substance. Scientists think the oil helps the dolphin swim fast.

Teeth

Sharks that hunt fish and other marine animals have rows and rows of very sharp teeth. The teeth often have a jagged edge, like a knife. This makes them even better at slicing through their prey. Sometimes a shark loses one of its teeth when it bites a fish. This is no problem for a shark. Behind each tooth is another one waiting to take its place!

It's amazing!

A shark uses more than 20,000 teeth in its lifetime. It can have up to 3,000 teeth in its mouth at any one time!

A great white shark has several rows of teeth. New teeth wait to replace any that fall out.

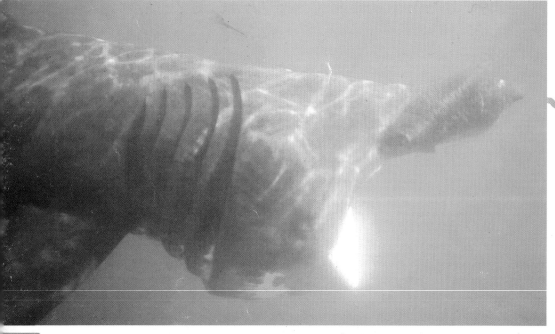

Not all sharks have teeth. This basking shark catches plankton on bristles that grow in its gills.

The common dolphin has up to 58 teeth. The teeth of most dolphins are like small, sharp spears. They are excellent for gripping fish that the dolphins catch. However, the teeth are not good for chewing, so dolphins have to swallow fish whole.

The Ganges river dolphin has long front teeth to snap up fish from the muddy river bottom.

It's amazing!

Dolphins usually eat fish head first. That way, the rough scales will not scratch the dolphin's throat!

The bottlenose dolphin has fewer teeth than the common dolphin and eats mainly cuttlefish.

Breathing

Sharks breathe by taking oxygen from water, not air. To help them do this, they have **gills** on each side of the head. Water goes into the shark's mouth as it swims. The water flows over the gills, which take out the oxygen. Most sharks have to keep moving to keep water flowing through their gills.

It's amazing!
Some sharks would die if they stopped swimming.

A gray nurse shark lives and feeds on the ocean floor.

gill slits

blowhole

Two Atlantic spotted dolphins swim to the surface for air.

Dolphins breathe by taking oxygen into their **lungs** from the air—just as we do. They swim to the surface and take in air through a blowhole, which is like a nostril on top of the head. By closing their blowholes, dolphins can hold their breath to dive underwater. Some dolphins can hold their breath for 15 minutes and dive more than 1,000 feet deep.

Finding Food

Most sharks eat fish, squid, and sometimes even dolphins. They find prey by using their incredible sense of smell. Sharks can smell the blood of an injured fish from several miles away. All animals send out tiny electrical charges. Some sharks have small "sensitive pits" on their nose that can pick up the charges. They can even find fish that are buried under the sand.

It's amazing!

A shark has such a good sense of smell that it can smell a single drop of blood in a 1,300-gallon tank of water!

Because they have sensitive pits, sharks can detect even weak electrical charges.

sensitive pits

A dolphin uses **sonar** to find its food. For this purpose, it has a special body organ in its head. Part of this organ, the "melon," makes clicking and whistling sounds called *sonar sound waves*. These waves bounce back from objects in their path to the dolphin, like an **echo**. The dolphin uses them to locate prey.

River dolphins use sonar to help them find food in dark, muddy water.

melon

Hunting

Some sharks hunt in schools. Once sharks have attacked their prey, the blood in the water may send them into a "feeding frenzy." They may bite anything they see—even each other!

The thresher shark uses its long tail to help it catch fish. It swims around the fish, herding them together with its tail, before moving in to eat them.

This young seal has survived a shark attack.

Gray reef sharks having a feeding frenzy.

Dolphins work together to hunt fish. Some species, like the common dolphin, herd schools of fish into shallow waters and charge at them. The charging makes a wave that washes the fish out of the water and onto the beach. The dolphins then throw themselves out of the water to snap up the fish!

A bottlenose dolphin hunts fish on a reef.

Babies

Most sharks give birth to live young, or small versions of themselves. However, some lay eggs. When a baby shark is born, it must take care of itself right away and avoid its enemies—especially other sharks!

Egg-laying sharks lay tough, leathery eggs. The baby shark grows in the egg, feeding off the nourishing **yolk** until it hatches.

A swell shark hatches from its egg.

the egg
hatching

It's amazing!
People who found shark eggs washed up on the beach used to call them "mermaid's purses" because they looked so strange.

All female dolphins give birth to live young. Female dolphins usually have one baby at a time. A baby dolphin can swim as soon as it is born. Its mother feeds it milk and protects it from enemies, especially sharks. The baby stays with its mother for three years. During that time, the mother and other female dolphins in the group look after it. When it is old enough to look after itself, it will stay with the group.

The bottlenose dolphin mother feeds her baby milk for about 18 months.

It's amazing!
Young dolphins learn while playing games. They make up games, such as tug-of-war with seaweed!

Fact File

Sharks

Largest
The whale shark can measure more than 50 feet and weigh 20 tons.

The largest meat-eating fish is the great white shark, which can grow up to 21 feet long.

Smallest
The spined pygmy shark is only 9 inches long.

Food
Basking and whale sharks have no teeth. They catch small animal and plant life called *plankton* in their gills.

Sharks with teeth eat seals, birds, porpoises, dolphins, and smaller fish, including other sharks.

The teeth and jaws of a great white shark.

22

Dolphins

Some dolphins can jump up to 20 feet above the water.

Largest
Killer whales can measure up to 33 feet and weigh several tons.

Smallest
Hector's dolphin grows to 4.8 feet long.

Food
Dolphins eat fish and squid. Killer whales also eat penguins, seals, porpoises, and other dolphins. They have even been known to attack other kinds of whales!

Glossary

camouflage colored or shaped in a way that makes an animal hard to see   9

coastal water the sea around the edge of a country   6

echo a sound that bounces back   17

gills parts of a fish that take oxygen from water   14

lungs organs of an animal that take oxygen from the air   15

prey an animal that is hunted by another animal for food   6

scales thin, hard plates that protect the fish   10

sonar a way of finding things underwater by sending out sounds and listening for the echo   17

species a group of living things that are very similar   4

streamlined shaped in a way to go fast   8

yolk a sac of food found in eggs   20

Index

Further Readings

Amato, Carol A. *The Truth About Sharks*. Barron's, 1995.

Hall, Howard. *Sharks: the Perfect Predators*. Silver Burdett Press, 1995.

Hoyt, Erich. *Riding With the Dolphins: the Equinox Guide to Dolphins and Porpoises*. Camden House, 1992.